In Mem

Thirty Poems of Bereavement

Candlestick Press

Published by:
Candlestick Press,
Diversity House, 72 Nottingham Road, Arnold, Nottingham UK NG5 6LF
www.candlestickpress.co.uk

Design and typesetting by Craig Twigg

Printed by Ratcliff & Roper Print Group, Nottinghamshire, UK

Illustration © Lizzie Adcock, www.arumliliedesigns.co.uk

Candlestick Press monogram © Barbara Shaw, 2008

© Candlestick Press, 2012

First Published 2012
Reprinted 2014
Second edition, revised 2018
Reprinted 2020

ISBN 978 1 907598 67 8

Acknowledgements:

The poems in this pamphlet are reprinted from the following books, all by permission of the publishers listed unless stated otherwise. Every effort has been made to trace the copyright holders of the poems published in this book. The editor and publisher apologise if any material has been included without permission or without the appropriate acknowledgement, and would be glad to be told of anyone who has not been consulted. Thanks are due to all the copyright holders cited below for their kind permission:

Peter Porter, excerpt from 'An Exequy' from *The Rest on the Flight: Selected Poems*, 2010, is reprinted by kind permission of Pan Macmillan, London. Copyright © Peter Porter, 2010; Dylan Thomas, 'And Death Shall Have No Dominion' is reprinted from *Collected Poems*, Orion, 2000; Paul Durcan, 'Staring Out The Window Three Weeks After His Death' from *Praise In Which I Live And Move And Have My Being*, Harvill Secker, 2012, is reprinted by kind permission of the author and was first published in *Poetry London*; Derek Mahon, 'Everything is Going to Be All Right' is reprinted by kind permission of the author and The Gallery Press, Loughcrew, Oldcastle, County Meath, Ireland from *New Collected Poems* (2011); Adrian Mitchell, 'Death Is Smaller Than I Thought' from *In Person: 30 Poets*, Bloodaxe Books, 2008, is reprinted by permission of United Agents on behalf of The Estate of Adrian Mitchell; Jackie Kay, 'Darling' is reprinted from *Darling: New and Selected Poems*, Bloodaxe Books, 2007; Wendy Cope, 'My Funeral' is reprinted from *Family Values*,

Where poets are no longer living, their dates are given.

Contents

Remember

Remember me when I am gone away,
   Gone far away into the silent land;
   When you can no more hold me by the hand,
Nor I half turn to go yet turning stay.
Remember me when no more day by day
   You tell me of our future that you planned:
   Only remember me; you understand
It will be late to counsel then or pray.
Yet if you should forget me for a while
   And afterwards remember, do not grieve:
   For if the darkness and corruption leave
   A vestige of the thoughts that once I had,
Better by far you should forget and smile
   Than that you should remember and be sad.

Christina Rossetti (1830 – 1894)

Wanderer's Night Song

O'er all the hilltops is quiet now,
In all the tree-tops hearest thou
Hardly a breath;

The birds are asleep in the trees;
Wait, wait - soon like these
Thou too shalt rest,
Thou too shalt rest.

Translated from Johann Wolfgang von Goethe (1749 – 1832)
by Henry Wadsworth Longfellow (1807 – 1882)

'don't tell me that I mourn too much'

don't tell me that I mourn too much
and I won't tell you that you mourn too much
don't tell me that I mourn too little
and I won't tell you that you mourn too little
don't tell me that I mourn in the wrong place
and I won't tell you that you mourn in the wrong place
don't tell me that I mourn at the wrong time
and I won't tell you that you mourn at the wrong time
don't tell me that I mourn in the wrong way
and I won't tell you that you mourn in the wrong way

I may get it wrong, I will get it wrong, I have got it wrong
but don't tell me.

Michael Rosen

The Dead

The dead are always looking down on us, they say,
while we are putting on our shoes or making a sandwich,
they are looking down through the glass-bottom boats of
   heaven
as they row themselves slowly through eternity.

They watch the tops of our heads moving below on earth,
and when we lie down in a field or on a couch,
drugged perhaps by the hum of a warm afternoon,
they think we are looking back at them,

which makes them lift their oars and fall silent
and wait, like parents, for us to close our eyes.

Billy Collins

The Baton

How smoothly you handed on the baton.
As if you'd known the time and place
and kept it secret from us; then
when the moment came, yielded it up
saying *Take it, quick, I cannot hold it,*
and let it swiftly slip your grasp.
We were left looking down at your empty hands,
the worn, surrendered fingers,
and a weight that had suddenly shifted.

Anna Wigley

Villanelle

When an ordinary man dies
Like that, all of a sudden,
There is no darkening of the skies,

Outside the lawns remain green and sodden
And vegetables pulled for supper lie
There is no sudden darkening of the sky

You can see the path his boots have trodden
The boots that slowly fold and subside
When an ordinary man dies

How ordinary! The cats still need feeding
The unbidden sun must endlessly rise
There is no sudden darkening of the skies

The shed is oven warm and full of flies
The beds grow and want weeding
When an ordinary man dies

It is a thing of great surprise
That no curtain is rent, no sacrifice lies bleeding
There is no sudden darkening of the skies

Only the ordinary parting with other lives
The barely audible tearing of ties
And no sudden darkening of the skies
When an ordinary man dies.

Sasha Dugdale

from **An Exequy**

The rooms and days we wandered through
Shrink in my mind to one – there you
Lie quite absorbed by peace – the calm
Which life could not provide is balm
In death. Unseen by me, you look
Past bed and stairs and half-read book
Eternally upon your home,
The end of pain, the left alone.
I have no friend, or intercessor,
No psychopomp or true confessor
But only you who know my heart
In every cramped and devious part –
Then take my hand and lead me out,
The sky is overcast by doubt,
The time has come, I listen for
Your words of comfort at the door,
O guide me through the shoals of fear –
'Fürchte dich nicht, ich bin bei dir.'*

Peter Porter (1929 – 2010)

*'Don't be afraid, I am with you'

Staring Out the Window Three Weeks After His Death

On the last day of his life as he lay comatose in the hospital bed
I saw that his soul was a hare which was poised
In the long grass of his body, ears pricked.
It sprang toward me and halted and I wondered if it
Could hear me breathing
Or if it could smell my own fear which was,
Could he but have known it, greater than his
For plainly he was a just and playful man
And just and playful men are as brave as they are rare.
Then his cancer-eroded body appeared to shudder
As if a gust of wind blew through the long grass
And the hare of his soul made a u-turn
And began bounding away from me
Until it disappeared from sight into a dark wood
And I thought – that is the end of that,
I will not be seeing him again.
He died in front of me, no one else was in the room.
My eyes teemed with tears, I could not damp them down.
I stood up to walk around his bed
Only to catch sight again of the hare of his soul
Springing out of the wood into a beachy cove of sunlight
And I thought – yes, that's how it is going to be from now on:
The hare of his soul always there, when I least expect it;
Popping up out of nowhere, sitting still.

Paul Durcan

Everything is Going to Be All Right

How should I not be glad to contemplate
the clouds clearing beyond the dormer window
and a high tide reflected on the ceiling?
There will be dying, there will be dying,
but there is no need to go into that.
The lines flow from the hand unbidden
and the hidden source is the watchful heart;
the sun rises in spite of everything
and the far cities are beautiful and bright.
I lie here in a riot of sunlight
watching the day break and the clouds flying.
Everything is going to be all right.

Derek Mahon

The Parting Glass

Oh all the time that e'er I spent,
I spent it in good company;
And any harm that e'er I've done,
I trust it was to none but me;
May those I've loved through all the years
Have memories now they'll e'er recall;
So fill to me the parting glass,
Goodnight, and joy be with you all.

Oh all the comrades that e'er I had,
Are sorry for my going away;
And all the loved ones that e'er I had
Would wish me one more day to stay.
But since it falls unto my lot
That I should leave and you should not,
I'll gently rise and I'll softly call
Goodnight, and joy be with you all.

Of all good times that e'er we shared,
I leave to you fond memory;
And for all the friendship that e'er we had
I ask you to remember me;
And when you sit and stories tell,
I'll be with you and help recall;
So fill to me the parting glass,
God bless, and joy be with you all.

Traditional Irish

from After the Green Gown of My Mother Gone Down

August, her large heart slows down then stops.
Fall now, and trees flame, catch a fire and riot

last leaves in scarlet and gold fever burning.
Remember when you heard Bob Marley hymn

'Redemption Song,' and from his tone and timbre
you sensed him traveling? He had sent the band home

and was just keeping himself company, cooling star,
sad rudeboy fretting on cowboy box guitar

in a studio with stray echo and wailing sound
lost singing scatting through the door of no return.

When the green goes, beloved, the secret is opened.
The breath falls still, the life covenant is broken.

Dress my mother's cold body in a deep green gown.
Catch a fire and let fall and flame time come,

after the green gown of my mother gone down.

Lorna Goodison

Death Is Smaller Than I Thought

My Mother and Father died some years ago
I loved them very much.
When they died my love for them
Did not vanish or fade away.
It stayed just about the same,
Only a sadder colour.
And I can feel their love for me,
Same as it ever was.

Nowadays, in good times or bad,
I sometimes ask my Mother and Father
To walk beside me or to sit with me
So we can talk together
Or be silent.

They always come to me.
I talk to them and listen to them
And think I hear them talk to me.
It's very simple –
Nothing to do with spiritualism
Or religion or mumbo jumbo.

It is imaginary.
It is real.
It is love.

Adrian Mitchell (1932 – 2008)

Darling

You might forget the exact sound of her voice
or how her face looked when sleeping.
You might forget the sound of her quiet weeping
curled into the shape of a half moon,

when smaller than her self, she seemed already to be leaving
before she left, when the blossom was on the trees
and the sun was out, and all seemed good in the world.
I held her hand and sang a song from when I was a girl –

Heel y'ho boys, let her go boys –
and when I stopped singing she had slipped away,
already a slip of a girl again, skipping off,
her heart light, her face almost smiling.

And what I didn't know or couldn't say then
was that she hadn't really gone.
The dead don't go till you do, loved ones.
The dead are still here holding our hands.

Jackie Kay

from 'For the Fallen'

They shall not grow old, as we that are left grow old:
    Age shall not weary them, nor the years condemn.
At the going down of the sun and in the morning
    We will remember them.

Laurence Binyon (1869 – 1943)

In Flanders Fields

In Flanders fields the poppies blow
Between the crosses, row on row,
That mark our place; and in the sky
The larks, still bravely singing, fly
Scarce heard amid the guns below.

We are the Dead. Short days ago
We lived, felt dawn, saw sunset glow,
Loved and were loved, and now we lie
In Flanders fields.

Take up our quarrel with the foe:
To you from failing hands we throw
The torch; be yours to hold it high.
If ye break faith with us who die
We shall not sleep, though poppies grow
In Flanders fields.

Lieutenant-Colonel John McCrae (1872 – 1918)

Vanished

She died, – this was the way she died;
And when her breath was done,
Took up her simple wardrobe
And started for the sun.

Her little figure at the gate
The angels must have spied,
Since I could never find her
Upon the mortal side.

Emily Dickinson (1830 – 1886)

Prayer

Let us be ears for the end of grass
the flickering, whispering grass,
the purple seeds carried like snow
beneath pylons, behind piers,
in late August or dry September.

Let us be mouths for the falling wind
thrumming, howling, then singing
through old fences and fairgrounds,
and in the first light let us be near
the stalled, the stuttering heart.

Let us be blessed in this house
with its emptinesses, its emptinesses —
let us attend to the passing
of small things: the lost nail,
the dropped stitch, the one pearl.

Faith Lawrence

Spring and Grief

I see my love in every little child
Whose eyes meet mine with laughter in their blue;
I hear him in the note, half sweet, half wild,
When bird calls bird their promise to renew;
I feel him in the ardor of the sun
That woos the fragrance from the waking flower,
And maple buds, rose flushed by beauty, won
To swift fulfilment of the Sun God's power.
The world is young once more as he was young,
With life and love reborn in everything –
O singing hearts! My own is faint and wrung;
The rapture and the riot of the Spring
Can but enhance the throb of my despair –
I miss him most when joy is everywhere!

Corinne Roosevelt Robinson (1861 – 1933)

Epitaph on a Child

Here, freed from pain, secure from misery, lies
A child, the darling of his parents' eyes;
A gentler lamb ne'er sported on the plain,
A fairer flower will never bloom again.
Few were the days allotted to his breath;
Now let him sleep in peace his night of death.

Thomas Gray (1716 – 1771)

Pink

white horses still their clattering feet
and wait for you
in shadow street their pink-plumed heads
stand straight for you
the lady at the bus-stop signs
a cross for you
the walker with the terrier dog
sighs loss for you
the traffic at the roundabout
must queue for you
the metronome of trotting hooves
beats true for you
the wagons on the carriageway
change gears for you
the rider on the cycle-path
wipes tears for you
pink rose-bay and foxgloves paint
July for you
the sunlight on the fell pours down
goodbye for you
the smiles of all who met you weave
the pall for you
that pink box in a white hearse is
too small for you
a sailing group of pink balloons
learn flight with you
and high the wings of wheeling birds
delight with you

Sue Millard

Epitaph on a Friend

An honest man here lies at rest,
The friend of man, the friend of truth,
The friend of age, and guide of youth:
Few hearts like his, with virtue warm'd,
Few heads with knowledge so inform'd;
If there's another world, he lives in bliss;
If there is none, he made the best of this.

Robert Burns (1759 – 1796)

Ode to My Brother

By ways remote and distant waters sped,
Brother, to thy sad graveside am I come,
That I may give the last gifts to the dead
And vainly parley with thine ashes dumb;
Since she who now bestows and now denies
Hath taken thee, hapless brother, from mine eyes.

But lo! these gifts, the heirlooms of past years,
Are made sad things to grace thy coffin shell,
Take them, all drenched with a brother's tears,
And, brother, for all time, hail and farewell.

Catullus (c.84 – c.54 BC)

Dirge without Music

I am not resigned to the shutting away of loving hearts in the
  hard ground.
So it is, and so it will be, for so it has been, time out of mind:
Into the darkness they go, the wise and the lovely. Crowned
With lilies and with laurel they go; but I am not resigned.

Lovers and thinkers, into the earth with you.
Be one with the dull, the indiscriminate dust.
A fragment of what you felt, of what you knew,
A formula, a phrase remains, – but the best is lost.

The answers quick & keen, the honest look, the laughter, the
  love, –
They are gone. They are gone to feed the roses. Elegant and
  curled
Is the blossom. Fragrant is the blossom. I know. But I do not
  approve.
More precious was the light in your eyes than all the roses of the
  world.

Down, down, down into the darkness of the grave
Gently they go, the beautiful, the tender, the kind;
Quietly they go, the intelligent, the witty, the brave
I know. But I do not approve. And I am not resigned.

Edna St. Vincent Millay (1892 – 1950)

My Funeral

I hope I can trust you, friends, not to use our relationship
As an excuse for an unsolicited ego-trip.
I have seen enough of them at funerals and they make
   me cross.
At this one, though deceased, I aim to be the boss.
If you are asked to talk about me for five minutes, please
   do not go on for eight.
There is a strict timetable at the crematorium and nobody
   wants to be late.
If invited to read a poem, just read the bloody poem.
   If requested
To sing a song, just sing it, as suggested,
And don't say anything. Though I will not be there,
Glancing pointedly at my watch and fixing the speaker
   with a malevolent stare,
Remember that this was how I always reacted
When I felt that anybody's speech, sermon or poetry reading
   was becoming too protracted.
Yes, I was impatient and intolerant, and not always polite
And if there aren't many people at my funeral, it will
   serve me right.

Wendy Cope

Funeral Blues

Stop all the clocks, cut off the telephone,
Prevent the dog from barking with a juicy bone,
Silence the pianos and with muffled drum
Bring out the coffin, let the mourners come.

Let aeroplanes circle moaning overhead
Scribbling on the sky the message He Is Dead,
Put crêpe bows round the white necks of the public doves,
Let the traffic policemen wear black cotton gloves.

He was my North, my South, my East and West,
My working week and my Sunday rest,
My noon, my midnight, my talk, my song;
I thought that love would last for ever: I was wrong.

The stars are not wanted now: put out every one;
Pack up the moon and dismantle the sun;
Pour away the ocean and sweep up the wood.
For nothing now can ever come to any good.

WH Auden (1907 – 1973)

Funeral Song from *Cymbeline*

Fear no more the heat o' the sun,
  Nor the furious winter's rages;
Thou thy worldly task has done,
  Home art gone and ta'en thy wages:
Golden lads and girls all must,
As chimney-sweepers, come to dust.

Fear no more the frown o' the great,
  Thou art past the tyrant's stroke;
Care no more to clothe and eat;
  To thee the reed is as the oak:
The sceptre, learning, physic, must
All follow this, and come to dust.

Fear no more the lightning-flash,
  Nor the all-dreaded thunder-stone;
Fear not slander, censure rash;
  Thou hast finish'd joy and moan:
All lovers young, all lovers must
Consign to thee, and come to dust.

No exorciser harm thee!
Nor no witchcraft charm thee!
Ghost unlaid forbear thee!
Nothing ill come near thee!
Quiet consummation have;
And renownèd be thy grave!

William Shakespeare (1564 – 1616)

Wintering

If I close my eyes I can picture him
flitting the hedgerow for splints
or a rib of wood to kindle the fire,

or reading the snow for whatever
it was that came out of the trees
and circled the house in the night;

if I listen I can hear him out
in the kitchen, scudding potatoes,
calling the cat in; if I breathe

I can smell the ghost of a fire,
a burning of leaves that would fizz
in the mizzle before snow.

There is in this house now
a stillness of cat fur and boxes,
of photographs, paperbacks, waste-

paper baskets; a lifetime
of things that I've come here
to winter or to burn.

There is in this world one snow fall.
Everything else is just weather.

Matthew Hollis

The Scattering

I cast you into the waters.
Be lake, or random moon.

Be first light,
lifting up its beggar's cup.

I scatter your ashes.
Be the gale teaching autumn
to mend its ways,
or leopard so proud of his spotted coat.

Be the mentor of cherry trees.

I cast your dust far and wide,
a sower broadcasting seed:
Be wild rose or hellebore or all-heal.

Descend as a vein of silver,
never to be seen,
deep in the lynx-eyed earth.

Rise as barn owl white as dusk;
dove or raven marvelling at his flight.
Know different delights.

Penelope Shuttle

And Death Shall Have No Dominion

And death shall have no dominion.
Dead men naked they shall be one
With the man in the wind and the west moon;
When their bones are picked clean and the clean bones gone,
They shall have stars at elbow and foot;
Though they go mad they shall be sane,
Though they sink through the sea they shall rise again;
Though lovers be lost love shall not;
And death shall have no dominion.

And death shall have no dominion.
Under the windings of the sea
They lying long shall not die windily;
Twisting on racks when sinews give way,
Strapped to a wheel, yet they shall not break;
Faith in their hands shall snap in two,
And the unicorn evils run them through;
Split all ends up they shan't crack;
And death shall have no dominion.

And death shall have no dominion.
No more may gulls cry at their ears
Or waves break loud on the seashores;
Where blew a flower may a flower no more
Lift its head to the blows of the rain;
Though they be mad and dead as nails
Heads of the characters hammer through daisies;
Break in the sun till the sun breaks down,
And death shall have no dominion.

Dylan Thomas (1914 – 1953)

Eulogy

Warm summer sun
    shine kindly here,
Warm Southern wind
    blow softly here,
Green sod above
    lie light, lie light –
Good night, dear heart,
    good night, good night.

Mark Twain (1835 – 1910) after Robert Richardson